Taste of America

By Melissa Whitcraft

CELEBRATION PRESS

Pearson Learning Group

Contents

Foods Around Us

Most supermarkets in the United States offer foods from all around the world. You can buy Mexican taco dinners, Italian spaghetti, and Chinese vegetables. German rye bread or African black-eyed peas are also available. These foods and many others show the different **ethnicities** of the American people.

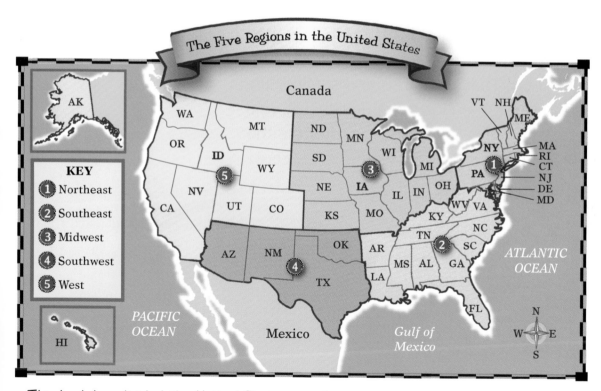

The Five Regions in the United States

KEY
1 Northeast
2 Southeast
3 Midwest
4 Southwest
5 West

Canada

Mexico

PACIFIC OCEAN

Gulf of Mexico

ATLANTIC OCEAN

This book has divided the United States into five regions.

Supermarkets also sell foods that are **indigenous** to the different regions that make up the United States. Indigenous foods come from plants or animals found in a particular geographic area. The climate and land affect the kinds of foods in a region. For example, the rich farmland in the Midwest is good for growing corn. The warm, sunny climate of the south is good for growing citrus fruits.

The location of a region also affects the types of foods found there. For example, regions near the coast depend on the seas for food. That's why fish and shellfish are popular in the Northeast, Southeast, and West regions. Indigenous foods were the main food sources for Native Americans long ago.

Food Facts

As American as apple pie is today, apples are not native to North America. The first trees were brought to New England by Pilgrim settlers from England.

Crabs are plentiful in the waters located in and near the Northeast and Southeast regions.

People from England began to settle in the United States in the 1600s. European settlers followed in the 1800s. Later, people from around the world settled in the United States. All these **immigrants** brought food and recipes from their native countries. They added the foods of the area to their cooking. Today most dishes are a mix of indigenous and **imported** foods. They are also made with recipes and cooking styles from around the world.

Between 1880 and 1930 more than 22 million people from Europe immigrated to the United States.

Indian Pudding

The Native Americans taught the settlers how to make a pudding using **cornmeal**. The settlers added molasses and sugar, which they had brought from their native countries. These ingredients made the pudding sweet. It became known as Indian Pudding. The pudding is still served today, often with sliced apples.

The Northeast

The Northeast Region

KEY
- ⊙ city
- lobster
- blue crab
- cranberries
- maple syrup
- grapes
- mushrooms
- blueberries
- tomatoes

Canada
ME
NH
VT
Plymouth
NY MA
CT RI
PA NJ
MD DE
ATLANTIC OCEAN

The Wampanoag (wahm-puh-NOH-ahg) were the first Native American people to live in the Northeast region. They survived by using handmade tools to hunt, fish, and farm. Wild animals, fish, berries, and nuts were indigenous to the Northeast. The Wampanoag planted corn, sweet potatoes, squash, and beans as other sources of food. They also discovered a way to **preserve** the fish they caught.

The Pilgrims arrived from England in 1620. They settled in Plymouth, Massachusetts. The Wampanoag taught the Pilgrims how to hunt, fish, and farm. They also showed them how to tap maple syrup from local trees.

The Wampanoag showed the Pilgrims where wild berries and nuts grew.

In the fall of 1621, the Pilgrims and Native Americans celebrated the first Thanksgiving.

The food the Pilgrims ate was very bland at first. They slowly added new foods and spices to their cooking. These ingredients added more flavor.

One favorite Pilgrim dish was baked beans. The Wampanoag introduced cooked beans to the Pilgrims. They simply cooked the beans in water over a low fire. Then the Pilgrims added salted pork and molasses. This dish is known today as Boston Baked Beans. It is often served with Boston Brown Bread, another dish first made by Pilgrims. This moist bread is made from flour, molasses, and raisins.

Molasses is thick, sweet syrup that settlers imported to add flavor to foods.

Thousands of Irish immigrants came to Boston in the mid-1840s. The potato crop in Ireland failed and farmers had no way to make a living. They had to leave Ireland or starve. The Irish used potatoes in many of their dishes. They added potatoes to the seafood and corn chowders when they arrived. Today, potatoes are one of the main ingredients in any **New England** chowder.

New England is known for its fresh seafood and chowders because of the variety of fish found in its coastal waters.

Lobster and potatoes are the two main ingredients in lobster chowder.

Italian immigrants settled in Boston in the 1880s. They added olive oil, tomatoes, green peppers, and garlic to the fish stews. These Italian ingredients changed the flavor of New England chowders yet again.

Italian immigrants also made pasta popular in the United States. Traditionally most Italians ate pasta with a little olive oil, cheese, and pepper. Italians started eating pasta with tomato sauce in the mid-1800s. Italian restaurants served meat with spaghetti in the United States. This pleased Americans who liked eating meat with their meals. That's how the Italian-American dish, spaghetti and meatballs, was created.

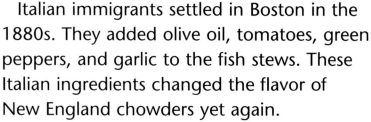

Pasta Takes Shape

The history of pasta goes back thousands of years. The earliest pasta was usually rolled into a long, flat form like lasagna. Beginning in the nineteenth century, new shapes and sizes of pasta could be made by machine. Thomas Jefferson brought the first pasta machine from Europe to the United States.

Italians also brought pizza to the United States. Pizza had been eaten in Italy for hundreds of years. The first pizzas in America were simple. They were made with dough, tomato sauce, and the herbs oregano and basil. The pizzas were also sprinkled with grated Italian cheese. Today, Americans can get almost any type of pizza they want. There is pizza with three cheeses or pizza with no cheese. Pizzas also come with a choice of toppings, including meat and vegetables.

Food Facts

About 3 billion pizzas are sold in the United States each year.

Pizza makes a quick and healthy meal.

The Southeast

The Native Americans in the Southeast survived on berries, nuts, wild animals, and seafood. They also planted peas, squash, onions, corn, and some fruit. Immigrants arrived to the Southeast and planted new crops and began raising animals for food.

English **colonists** settled in the Southeast in the early 1600s. They built large **plantations**. Enslaved Africans were the plantation cooks until slavery was ended in 1865. They prepared several dishes, including collard greens, **succotash**, and hominy. Hominy came from a local Native American custom. They cooked corn kernels until they were soft. Plantation cooks added milk, cream, eggs, and butter.

The Southeast Region

WV
VA
KY
Mississippi River
TN
NC
AR
SC
MS
AL
GA
LA
ATLANTIC OCEAN
New Orleans
Gulf of Mexico
FL

KEY

- city
- peanuts and pecans
- peaches
- shrimp
- blue crab
- rice
- citrus
- fish

Since the Spanish brought orange trees to Florida in the early 1500s, Florida has become the main producer of oranges.

Enslaved Africans prepared a variety of dishes in plantation kitchens, like the one above.

African cooks also used black-eyed peas they had brought from Africa. They added local rice and salted pork to create a dish called Hoppin-Jack. This dish is still popular in the Southeast today.

Smoked ham was also served on plantations. Before refrigeration, ham was smoked to keep it from spoiling. Today, smoked ham is often the centerpiece at holiday dinners.

fried chicken

Fried chicken was another popular dish in the Southeast in the nineteenth century. Often the chicken was served with hot biscuits. Today southern fried chicken is served in homes and restaurants everywhere.

The French first settled in New Orleans, Louisiana, in 1718. New Orleans became Spanish when Spain took over the city in 1764. The French and Spanish settlers created another southeastern **cuisine**.

Creole cooking became popular with wealthy French and Spanish traders who lived in New Orleans. The spicy mix of ingredients included local meat and seafood. Spanish green peppers and tomatoes were used for seasoning. The sauces were French. An African vegetable called okra was used to thicken Creole sauces.

A New Orleans restaurant owner holds a plate of Cajun food.

Cajun cooking is similar to Creole cooking. Cajun food was developed by the French colonists known as Acadians. They left Canada and settled on the Mississippi River near New Orleans in 1775.

Cajun cooks also used local meat and seafood in their cooking. They added homegrown onions, rice, and hot peppers for flavor. Their one-pot meals made the most of what the land offered. Cajun and Creole dishes are popular today in restaurants across the United States.

Food Facts

In 1920, automobile inventor Henry Ford invented the charcoal briquette for barbecuing.

Southern Barbecue

When we think of southern food, we can't forget the barbecue, which is thought to have started in the South. True barbecuing is the process of cooking meat at a low temperature for a long time over wood coals. Today, when most Americans barbecue they are actually cooking food over a grill heated by charcoal or gas.

The Midwest

Pioneers moved to the Midwest in the 1800s. They were looking for more land to farm. Some of these settlers came from eastern states. Others came from Europe.

Farmers from Switzerland settled in Wisconsin in the 1840s. They changed forests into farms and raised dairy cows. They made cheese and butter from milk. They also made traditional Swiss cheese pies called quiches. Quiches were made from eggs, cheese, bacon, and onion.

The Midwest Region

Canada

ND
MN
WI
MI
SD
Great Plains
Central Plains
NE
IA
IL
IN
OH
KS
MO

KEY

- grain
- cherries
- pigs
- beef cattle
- corn
- dairy cattle

Dairy farming is a major industry in the Midwest.

Once the buffalo hunting lands of the Sioux Native Americans, the Great Plains began producing America's wheat in the 1850s.

More European immigrants arrived throughout the mid to late nineteenth century. People from Denmark, Sweden, and Norway settled in the Midwest. These immigrants changed more of the land into farms. They planted fields of wheat, rye, and other grains. The Great Plains became known as America's "breadbasket."

Many American baking traditions came out of this period. Immigrants introduced pancakes and holiday cookies cut into festive shapes. Nuts, sugar, candied fruit, and raisins were needed to make special holiday cookies. These ingredients were difficult to buy, so **pioneer** women saved up the ingredients during the year.

Wheat farmers from Germany settled in the Midwest in the 1880s. They also added their own baking traditions. They opened bakeries where they sold homemade wheat, rye, and pumpernickel bread. German immigrants also sold jelly donuts, cookies, and apple strudel. Strudel is a dessert made by cooking fruit and sugar in a flaky pastry crust. The bakeries became a place for customers to eat, drink, and talk with neighbors.

The local bakery shop is often a popular meeting place.

German immigrants are most famous for introducing hamburgers and hot dogs to Americans. German cooks first pounded beef into patties in Hamburg, Germany. That was in the early 1800s. The patties were called Hamburg meat, or hamburgers.

Cooks started serving hamburgers and hot dogs with rolls in the late 1800s. People working in cities were looking for a quick and less-filling lunch. Hot dogs with rolls were the perfect meals on the run for these workers. Today these meals on the run are often called fast foods.

Food Facts

Originally, some hot dogs were called dachshund sausages because they looked like the dachshund dog. By 1901, they became hot dogs because when first cooked, they were too hot to handle without a bun.

dachsund

A variety of fast foods are available—from lo mein to hamburgers.

The Southwest

The Pueblo Native Americans of the Southwest survived on the indigenous foods of the region. They hunted wild turkey and other animals. The Pueblos also planted crops, such as pinto beans, squash, and corn that could survive in the hot, dry climate. The corn had long roots which reached down to the damp soil below the surface.

The Spanish arrived to the Southwest in the 1540s. They introduced many of their own crops to the region. They grew oranges, limes, onions, carrots, eggplants, and lentils. The Spaniards used **irrigation** techniques first used by the Pueblos.

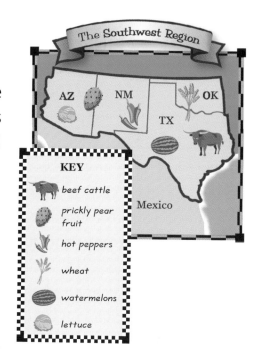

The Southwest Region

AZ
NM
OK
TX

Mexico

KEY

beef cattle

prickly pear fruit

hot peppers

wheat

watermelons

lettuce

yellow onion

lentils

eggplant

The Spanish brought other foods to the Southwest. Hot peppers were carried from the Aztecs in South America and tortillas from Mexico. The Spanish also brought different animals, such as pigs, goats, and chickens. These animals were raised for their meats. Goats also provided milk for the Spaniards to make cheese.

All these different ingredients were blended together over time. Spanish cooks mixed Native American pinto beans with meat to make *chili con carne*. They also rolled and filled *tortillas* with grated cheese, onion, and meat. This dish is called *enchiladas*. The Spaniards added hot pepper sauce to their foods for spice.

Flattened Bread

The Spanish brought *tortillas*, or "little cakes," from a Native American nation in Mexico. They were made from flattened corn paste. *Tortillas* were flat and soft bread that were also used as spoons or plates.

In the nineteenth century, cowboys moved herds of up to 3,000 cattle north at any one time.

The Spanish also introduced cattle to the Southwest. The dry land was perfect for grazing animals. The Spanish built farms and raised cattle for their beef. They rode around their large ranches on horses they had brought from Spain.

American pioneers from the East started building cattle ranches by the mid-1880s. Cowboys moved the cattle north to be sold during each spring. They rode horses to drive, or move, the cattle along. Sometimes they traveled more than 700 miles on a cattle drive. The length of the trip changed depending on the weather. A drive could take anywhere from twenty-five to one hundred days.

Moving the cattle north was difficult work. Cowboys traveled with a cook and a food wagon called a chuck wagon. The cooks prepared meals for the cowboys. They often didn't have fresh foods because they were out on the trail for so long.

Chuck wagon beans were popular while on the trail. Cooks made this dish by cooking pinto beans with onions, garlic, and salt pork. Chuck wagon beans were served over biscuits with a sprinkle of hot pepper powder for flavor. Cooks also made fajitas. This dish was made from strips of barbecued beef or other meat.

The chuck wagon was filled with enough cooking equipment and supplies to last the length of the cattle drive.

Dried Meat Snack

The cowboys ate dried, smoked strips of beef while out on the trail. They learned this from the Sioux who carried dried, smoked buffalo meat on their hunts. The Spanish called these strips *charqui*. Today, we know this snack as beef jerky.

beef fajita

Today, many of these southwestern cowboy dishes are described as Tex-Mex. These foods combine flavors and ingredients popular in both Texas and Mexico. Some dishes are made with a mix of beans and peppers. Other dishes are a mix of shredded meats served with corn *tortillas*. Many southwestern dishes show how Mexican, Spanish, and pioneer foods blend together.

jalepeño pepper

A variety of sauces are used to add flavor to Southwestern Barbecue.

The West

The first immigrants to settle in California were the Spanish. They started building **missions** on the West Coast in 1769. The Spaniards introduced many vegetables and fruits to the region.

The mild climate in the valleys reminded the immigrants of Spain. They planted onions, garlic, and carrots. They also introduced grapes, olives, and artichokes to the region. In the southern region, they planted oranges, mangoes, papayas, and apricots.

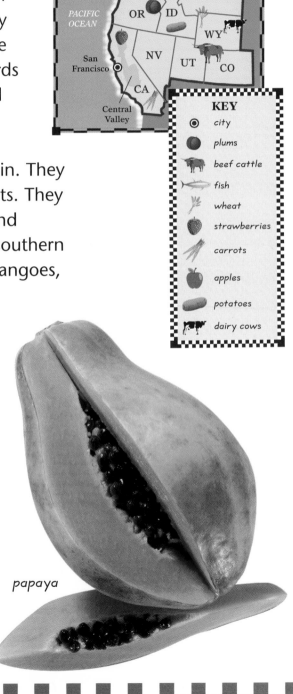

The West Region

Canada

PACIFIC OCEAN

WA
OR
ID
MT
WY
NV
UT
CO
CA

San Francisco

Central Valley

KEY

- ◉ city
- plums
- beef cattle
- fish
- wheat
- strawberries
- carrots
- apples
- potatoes
- dairy cows

artichoke

papaya

People from around the world flocked to California in 1848 for the gold rush. People were drawn again in the 1860s to build the railroad. Foods from different immigrants were blended to create new American dishes.

The Chinese laborers in California planted Chinese vegetables. They included bok choy, snow peas, and cabbage. The Chinese used local and Chinese foods to make noodle and rice dishes. Chinese cooking traditions and foods didn't gain popularity until the 1920s. Today, Chinese restaurants serve a variety of dishes, including chow mein, dumplings, and fried rice. Many blend two or more ingredients introduced by different immigrant groups.

egg rolls

Chinese Stir-fry

Chinese immigrants introduced stir-fried cooking to the West. The Chinese were used to cooking their foods quickly because there was limited fuel in their native country. The Chinese used thinly sliced meats and vegetables, and quickly fried the ingredients in a hot pan called a *wok*.

Central Valley, California became a thriving farm area in the 1940s. The farmland covered approximately 400 miles. Immigrants from Mexico came to work on the farms. Their traditional foods influenced California cooking.

Immigrants arrived from Italy, Greece, and Portugal in the mid to late 1800s. They settled in Central Valley. These European immigrants planted fields of vegetables. They included artichokes, lettuce, broccoli, and peppers. Foods from their native countries, such as olive oil, garlic, cheese, basil, and oregano were added to make flavorful dishes.

Farmers in the Central Valley started canning their produce at the end of the 1800s. Fruits and vegetables could now be shipped great distances without spoiling. Families across the United States could enjoy foods introduced by European immigrants.

Today, fields of vegetables spread out as far as the eye can see. The citrus groves planted by the Spanish continue to thrive. Many of the fruits and vegetables grown in California are shipped to supermarkets and restaurants around the country.

Workers harvest a lettuce field in California.

Foods of Today

   Each of the five regions in the United States developed its own ethnic foods. People who settled in each region changed the foods over time. Today, the geographic borders that separated these regions no longer exist. Americans living in any U.S. region can enjoy foods from almost any part of the world. For example, Southwestern fajitas are found in restaurants across the United States.

Many Americans enjoy sampling the growing number of foods offered at restaurants.

Ethnic foods continue to change as new groups of people settle in the United States. Asian food is no longer simply Chinese. Since the mid-1900s, immigrants from several areas of Asia have introduced their cuisines. Vietnamese, Thai, Korean, and Japanese foods are becoming more popular. Immigrants from India and Pakistan have also introduced native cooking traditions and foods. Finally, modern travel and technology continue to add spice and flavor to American foods.

A waitress displays Thai dishes which include a mix of noodles, vegetables, meat, seafood, and spices.

Foods Across Time

tortillas
eggplant
jalepeños

Succotash
hominy
okra

molasses
baked beans
brown bread

**1540s:
Southwest**

Spanish settle

**1600s:
Southeast**

Enslaved
Africans arrive

**1620:
Northeast**

Pilgrims settle